21st Century Skills **INNOVATION** *Library*

Trucks

by Matt Mullins

INNOVATION IN TRANSPORTATION

Published in the United States of America by Cherry Lake Publishing
Ann Arbor, Michigan
www.cherrylakepublishing.com

Content Adviser: Amy C. Newman, Director, Forney Museum of Transportation

Design: The Design Lab

Photo Credits: Cover and page 3, ©Gary Blakeley, used under license from Shutterstock, Inc.; page 4, ©vadim kozlovsky, used under license from Shutterstock, Inc.; page 5, ©Fernando Rodrigues, used under license from Shutterstock, Inc.; page 7, ©Arthur Eugene Preston, used under license from Shutterstock, Inc.; page 8, ©iStockphoto.com/gocosmonaut; page 10, ©Robert Kyllo, used under license from Shutterstock, Inc.; page 13, ©JoLin, used under license from Shutterstock, Inc.; page 15, ©Peter Treanor/ Alamy; page 17, ©Nancy Brammer, used under license from Shutterstock, Inc.; page 18, ©bygonetimes/ Alamy; page 21, ©AGStockUSA, Inc./Alamy; page 23, ©Ambient Images Inc./Alamy; page 25, ©AP Photo/HO/Mercedes Benz; page 27, ©AP Photo/HO/Krupp; page 29, ©AP Photo/Mark Duncan, file

Library of Congress Cataloging-in-Publication Data
Mullins, Matt.
Trucks / by Matt Mullins.
    p. cm.–(Innovation in transportation)
Includes index.
ISBN-13: 978-1-60279-237-1
ISBN-10: 1-60279-237-2
1. Trucking–History–Juvenile literature. 2. Trucks–History–Juvenile
literature. 3. Truck industry–History–Juvenile literature. I. Title. II.
Series.
HE5611.M85 2009
388.3'44–dc22   2008006746

Cherry Lake Publishing would like to acknowledge the work of
The Partnership for 21st Century Skills.
Please visit www.21stcenturyskills.org for more information.

CONTENTS

INNOVATION IN TRANSPORTATION

CHAPTER ONE

From Steam to Gas Power

Garbage trucks are just one kind of truck used by people around the world.

The garbage truck hauling away trash, the bus taking you to school, the semi cruising on the highway, and the pickup towing a ski boat—these are some of today's most common types of trucks. They carry people or goods or both. It is hard to imagine life without them. Most can travel at a quick speed. They can maneuver through streets carrying thousands of pounds of cargo.

Semi trucks are big, powerful machines that carry tons of goods over long distances.

Trucks haven't always been big and powerful. In 1769, French army engineer Nicholas Joseph Cugnot built a steam-powered vehicle for carrying cannons. It only moved at walking speed. His second version traveled at a little more than 10 miles (16 kilometers) an hour.

Cugnot's innovation did not look much like today's trucks. It was a three-wheeled wooden cart. Ahead of the front wheel hung a large steam kettle. As the water in it was heated to a boil, steam was formed. As the steam expanded, it pushed rods that pedaled the front wheel. With the giant boiler in front, Cugnot's truck was prone to tipping forward. It also ran out of steam every 15 or 20 minutes. When it did, he had to add water to the boiler, refire the wood, and wait for steam to build up. Then he'd resume driving.

Throughout the 1800s, the technology for steam-powered vehicles improved. Steam wagons carrying lumber, textiles, and other cargo appeared in England, France, Germany, the United States, and elsewhere. They were big and noisy. These "land locomotives" spooked horses and startled people who were out on walks. Determined inventors, engineers, and scientists found ways to make smaller **engines** that were still powerful.

In 1896, Gottlieb Daimler in Stuttgart, Germany, sold a four-wheeled, gas-powered vehicle designed to carry 3,300 pounds (1,497 kilograms) of cargo. It was the first manufactured motortruck. Within a decade or so, companies in Britain, France, and the United States started producing trucks. In 1907, International Harvester introduced its Auto Wagon, which some consider the **forerunner** to the pickup truck.

Still, merchants favored trains as the way to move goods. The United States and Europe already had rails. Steam locomotives chugged to every big city. They pulled dozens of train cars full of supplies and passengers for hundreds of miles. The railroad was simply the way freight was moved.

This view started to change during and after World War I (1914–1918). People began to realize how useful trucks could be. Trucks helped troops respond quickly

Soldiers use trucks for many purposes. Military trucks need to be tough enough to travel over all kinds of terrain.

The interstate highway system provides commuters and professional truck drivers with smooth roads. These roads make transportation much easier.

to sudden shifts in battle. Military and business leaders began to recognize the fact that trucks allowed more **flexibility** in moving goods than railroads. Unlike the railroad, trucks could move products across a state or simply around a corner. The problem with trucks was that some nations didn't have a good system of roadways.

This included the United States. The roads it had were often pitted and rutted dirt and gravel surfaces.

Then in 1956, the Federal-Aid Highway Act began to **remedy** the country's roadways. President Dwight D. Eisenhower had served as a general in the U.S. military during World War II (1939–1945). He had admired the sophisticated German highway system, the *autobahn*. Eisenhower wanted to create interstate highways so military trucks could move quickly from city to city in case of an enemy attack. Construction crews built interstates made of asphalt and concrete all over the country. They helped the U.S. economy expand rapidly. Great Britain passed a similar law in 1959.

Soon trucks became essential for moving goods around the country. Today, trucks carry more than half the products and materials that U.S. businesses move from city to city.

Learning & Innovation Skills

Trucks are self-moving, or automotive, vehicles that carry passengers and goods. Buses can be considered trucks because passengers are their payload (cargo that generates income for bus owners). A van is a little trickier. Maybe it's a car when it carries families, but a truck when it carries tomatoes to sell at a market.

Do you think a sport-utility vehicle (SUV) is a truck or a car? What do you think automobile manufacturers consider SUVs? Why?

CHAPTER TWO

The Fast Lane for Freight Hauling

The internal combustion engines in semi trucks have to create enough power to move the heavy vehicles plus the cargo they carry.

Innovation has always driven truck design. When people bought the first cars, they would often "fix" them to suit their needs. Trucks were converted to delivery vans, buses, and farm equipment. But certain inventions have profoundly influenced the development of the trucking industry.

The gas-powered **internal combustion engine** burns a mixture of gasoline and air. This is a more powerful energy source than the steam and electricity used in most 19th-century vehicles. Internal combustion made long-distance driving possible. It eliminated the need to stop every 15 minutes to take on more water to replace the used steam or to refire the motor.

An internal combustion engine burns (or combusts) its fuel inside itself (that is, internally). Its **ingenuity** lies in its method of harnessing the energy of combustion with cylinders and pistons.

Imagine you have a small wire spring. Stand it on a table, push it down lightly with your finger, and then quickly remove your finger. What happens? It springs back into shape so fast it bounces. Do it again but press harder, and the spring bounces higher. The harder you press down, or compress, the spring, the more powerfully it reacts.

The internal combustion engine does the same kind of thing, but its spring is a mixture of liquid gasoline and air, and its finger is a piston. The piston is a metal piece that slides snugly inside a metal tube, or cylinder. The engine sprays a mixture of air and gasoline into the cylinder. From the other end, the piston compresses the gas like your finger compressed the spring. A wire in the cylinder lets out a spark, igniting the tightly squeezed gas. The gas burns so quickly that it explodes and shoots the piston out.

In 1876, Nikolaus Otto designed an engine that compressed gas using pistons connected to the moving parts of manufacturing equipment. By burning the gas, the motor forced pistons into motion and machinery into action. A few years later, Karl Benz adjusted the design. He built a small gas-powered engine and used it to turn the wheels of his Motorwagen, the first vehicle powered by an internal combustion engine. Soon after, Rudolf Diesel designed a more **efficient** internal combustion engine that bears his name. Most commercial trucks today have **diesel engines**.

Over the years, engineers further improved **compression** in engines. They also found better ways to transfer power from engines to wheels. As engines became more powerful, trucks could haul more weight. They got faster, and delivery times became shorter.

The most recognizable **commercial** truck on the road is almost more tractor than truck. The semitruck is otherwise known as a tractor-trailer because, like a tractor, it pulls equipment to do a job. That equipment is the semitrailer. A trailer without front wheels, the semitrailer connects with a pin to a doughnut-shaped metal **coupler** on the back of a truck.

In 1914, Detroit blacksmith August Fruehauf began a trailer-manufacturing business. He built a semitrailer for a lumber merchant who had fitted his truck with

A semitrailer sits outside a loading dock. Semitrailers are connected to semitrucks with pins that connect to metal couplers on the backs of trucks.

a coupler. With several Fruehauf semitrailers and one tractor-trailer, a company could operate more efficiently because the truck could always be hauling cargo. There would be no need to wait—and waste time—during loading and unloading.

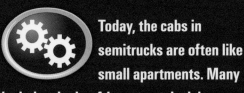
Semitrailers separated cargo from trucks and eventually helped truck drivers become their own bosses. Businesses no longer had to buy trucks and hire drivers. They could hire a truck owner to pick up a semitrailer and haul it off to a customer or warehouse in another city. The truck owner-operator could drop the trailer off at its destination, pick up a different trailer, and pull that cargo to yet another city.

Another innovation in trucks made it possible for perishable foods to be transported more easily and over longer distances. Meat and dairy products spoil quickly if they aren't kept cold, and many fresh fruits and vegetables don't hold up after hours in the heat. The development of refrigerated semitrailers, sometimes called reefers, meant that these foodstuffs could be safely shipped anywhere a truck could travel.

Frederick Jones is credited with developing the first widely used automatic refrigeration system for long-haul trucks in 1935. Before this time, many people had designed systems for keeping items cool during shipping. Some were as simple as packing containers with ice. Refrigerated railroad cars had been used since the

1840s. But Jones's design was smaller and could handle the shocks of road travel better than earlier designs. This technology expanded the trucking industry's reach because it allowed trucks to ship more types of goods.

Refrigerated semtrailers make it possible for milk and other perishable goods to be transported for long distances without spoiling.

CHAPTER THREE

The Business of Making and Using Trucks

Almost the moment they saw Benz's Motorwagen zipping around Mannheim, Germany, businessmen began considering how to use this new technology. Specialty trucks sprang up around Europe and the United States almost as fast as engineers could think them up.

John and Gus Mack sold a gas-powered, four-cylinder bus to a sightseeing company in 1900. It was the first American bus and carried 20 passengers. By 1911, the Mack Brothers Company had 825 employees in New York City. They built fire trucks, gravel-hauling trucks, and other heavy-duty vehicles.

In 1916, Ernest Holmes attached a chain to his car and pulled a friend's car from a creek. A few years later, the Ernest Holmes Company of Tennessee was manufacturing towing trucks. Creative thinkers in the

Tow trucks are often used to move cars that have been damaged in crashes.

1920s produced tanker trucks for carrying petroleum, repair trucks carrying towers to reach power lines, and trucks with containers that could be tilted to dump coal. British garbage collection trucks began appearing during this decade as well.

But the innovations of an automobile manufacturer in Detroit would soon change the way trucks, and most products, would be made in many parts of the world.

The first Ford Model Ts sold in 1908 for almost $900. Henry Ford was devoted to making his Model T

Henry Ford's Model T was the first mass-produced automobile. Most vehicles, including trucks, are now manufactured on assembly lines.

more affordable. To achieve this, he was convinced he had to improve manufacturing processes. By speeding up production, he would be able to reduce the cost of the automobiles.

In 1910, the Ford Motor Company moved into an 80-acre (32 hectares) factory. There Ford carefully designed factory space and machinery. Tracks brought railroad cars carrying ore right into the iron-making forges. Conveyor belts carried the Model T chassis (the frame and working parts of the vehicle, but not its body) along an assembly line, bringing the work to the workers. Instead of having only a few individuals with enough knowledge and skill to produce an entire car, each worker along the line was trained to do one task.

This approach to building cars meant that it didn't cost as much to train employees. Each employee only had to learn one step in the process of building a car. The assembly line also allowed vehicles to be produced much faster. Early Ford models required more than 12 hours to build. By 1925, a Model T rolled off the assembly line every 30 seconds—and sold for $290.

Other industries took notice. Many small manufacturers joined forces to create larger companies, so they could build factories using Ford's principles. Assembly lines were soon building trucks, airplanes, and many other products. But these factories were put to the test even in their early days, when demand for many items increased because of war.

When World War I began in 1914, generals expected railroads to be a key to success. They were a fast way to move supplies and troops over long distances. Trucks, they thought, would support trains and ships by carrying cargo to soldiers in the field. But the fighting revealed advantages that trucks had over railroads.

Life & Career Skills

Smooth, durable highways save drivers time and fuel. Maintaining and repairing roads can require a lot of resources. Replacing pavement can create a lot of waste. Engineers and highway designers are finding ways to use materials that last longer and are easier on the environment. Sometimes they grind up and reuse old pavement. They can also use industrial waste such as ash from iron factories that otherwise would end up in the trash. Keeping ash and old roads out of garbage dumps is important. It is just one way that highway designers, builders, and scientists act responsibly and help the communities in which they work.

Trucks didn't need rails. Sometimes they didn't even require *roads*. And they could be redesigned or reconfigured for different tasks. Armies carried big, heavy guns on four-wheel-drive trucks that could handle pitted battlefields and rough country. A French fortress survived a seven-month German attack even though it was cut off from a railroad line. They survived because soldiers and supplies were trucked in via a winding, gravel back road.

World War II, which started in Europe in 1939, increased truck use and innovation in similar fashion. It also influenced post-war truck use in North America, Europe, and Asia.

In 1956, the U.S. Congress and President Eisenhower passed the Federal-Aid Highway Act. It was commonly known as the National Interstate and Defense Highways Act because the government's plan was to create a network of roadways for the military to use in case of attack. But the armed forces were not the only ones using the highways.

Truckloads of grapefruit and oranges will be made into juice at this factory.

Businesses benefited at least as much as the armed forces from interstates. It became easy to truck oranges from Florida and coal from West Virginia around the country. The truck became the king of the road. Manufacturers made trucks larger, trailers longer, and motors stronger. At the same time, Americans grew wealthier, populations climbed, and cities spread out. Trucks brought food, clothes, and practically everything else to the suburbs.

CHAPTER FOUR

The Road Ahead

Fuel efficiency is at the heart of many trucking innovations on the horizon. According to the American Trucking Association, the U.S. trucking industry burns billions of gallons of fuel each year. Gasoline and diesel fuel both contribute to global warming and poor air quality. Any improvements that reduce the amount of fuel used by a motor will save the trucker money and help reduce pollution.

Hybrid vehicles use two motor systems: one electric, the other fuel-based. Battery-powered electric motors burn cleanly. Hybrid vehicles simply switch from one energy source to the other, based on how the system is configured and whether the vehicle is idling or accelerating. A U.S. company expects to sell the first hybrid semitruck in 2010.

A county dump in Pennsylvania is working on a way to convert methane gas into fuel for garbage trucks. As garbage decays in a landfill, it releases methane. The county already has machinery that generates electricity from the landfill methane. A methane-to-fuel system might produce 5,000 gallons (18,927 liter) of truck fuel a day. Garbage trucks would be collecting and dumping their own fuel source.

Biodiesel is fuel for diesel engines that is usually made from vegetables. Burning biodiesel produces less pollution than burning gasoline or crude oil–based diesel. Biodiesel can be made from plant oils, such as those from corn, soybeans, or rapeseeds. Used cooking oil from restaurants and food-processing plants can also be made into biodiesel.

Safeway, a grocery store chain based in California, has converted its fleet to biodiesel. Some national trucking

Using biodiesel fuel is just one way that trucking companies are trying to reduce air pollution.

DIAMOND PATH MEDIA CENTER
ISD No. 196

TRANSPORTATION

Learning & Innovation Skills

Some fuels may make sense to *use* but not to *produce*. Biodiesel and ethanol, which is made from corn, burn more cleanly than gas or regular diesel. Their emissions do less harm to the atmosphere, contributing less to global warming.

But these fuels require farming. Growing crops to make enough fuel for millions of vehicles may lead to serious environmental damage. What land will it be grown on? What problems do you think this kind of farming might create?

companies have begun using biodiesel for long-distance hauling. We may see a day when truckers pull up to restaurants to fill their stomachs and their gas tanks.

Some scientists believe that if trucks could drive themselves, traffic would improve through better use of highway space. Trucks are so heavy, and human reaction time so slow, that truckers often leave 100 feet (30 meters) or more between their trucks and the vehicles ahead, in case they need to stop suddenly.

There are scientists developing automatically controlled truck systems that would put computers at the wheel. With the help of **satellites**, radar, and sensors in the pavement, a computer could "watch" traffic and wirelessly control many trucks at once. The computer could sense changes in conditions and know to brake much quicker than a human. This would cut down on the amount of space needed between trucks. By driving closer together, trucks would free up space for other traffic.

Key Innovators

Innovation and historical change rarely occur in a flash. Even when driven by brilliant, creative engineers and designers, new machines may not be adopted immediately. Here are some notable innovators.

Karl Benz

Karl Friedrich Benz was born in Karlsruhe, Germany. He entered the university to study mechanical engineering at age 15 and received his

Karl Benz wasn't just a brilliant engineer. He was also a smart businessman.

diploma when he was 19. He began selling the Benz Patent Motorwagen in 1888. Part of Benz's genius was his clever use of **patents**. By securing several patents, he guaranteed himself financial control of his designs for several years. He first patented his motor in 1879 and then continued to improve it until he patented his automobile in 1886. During his work on the engine, he patented a number of mechanisms that support the engine, including a spark plug, radiator, and steering mechanism.

Soon after Gottlieb Daimler sold the first motor-truck in 1896, Benz sold a light delivery truck. A few years later, he introduced a heavy-duty truck. In 1926, Daimler's and Benz's companies merged, producing a line of cars and trucks under the name Mercedes-Benz.

Rudolf Diesel

Rudolf Diesel was born in Paris, France. As a young man, he studied engineering in Munich, Germany. Diesel thought steam engines and the Benz motor were inefficient. In each, only about 10 percent of the energy used moved the motor, and the rest was given off as heat. He developed a more efficient engine that used the heat generated by compressed air. Diesel built a motor that added fuel to a cylinder when the highly compressed air was hot enough to ignite fuel. He continued to improve

WELCHER IN ALLER WELT
GENANNT WIRD, ARBEITET
ÜNDUNG DES EINGESPRITZ-
BRENNSTOFFES.

DER MOTOR ÜBERTRAF DURCI
DICHTUNG DER VERBRENNUNG
ANDEREN WÄRMEKRAFTMAS
THERMISCHER WIRTSCHAFT

RUDOLF DIESEL
GEB. AM 18. MÄRZ 1858   GEST. AM 30. SEPT. 1913.

ER SCHUF GEMEINSAM MIT DER MASCHINENFABR
FRIED. KRUPP IN DEN JAHREN 1893 - 189

Rudolf Diesel invented the engine used in most commercial trucks on the road today.

his design. In 1898, he demonstrated his efficient new motor in Paris.

The diesel engine became popular for trucks in the 1930s because it uses much less fuel than the gasoline engine. Most commercial trucks today have diesel motors.

21st Century Content

In 1965, Ralph Nader's book *Unsafe at Any Speed* criticized an automotive corporation for a design that provided power at the expense of safety. It led the U.S. Congress to regulate consumer safety and push the auto industry toward innovations such as air bags and skid-free braking.

As a citizen, when you see something in society that concerns you, what can you do about it? What actions have you seen ordinary citizens take that have made a difference?

Ernest D. Swinton

One month before World War I began, British army officer Ernest D. Swinton received a letter from a friend. The letter described an American "caterpillar" tractor that rode on tracklike treads—bands of wood and chain that turned around a row of wheels.

Swinton thought such a machine would be useful in battle. He drafted plans for an armor-plated caterpillar truck fixed with two large guns. He presented them to his superiors in June 1915.

The Royal Navy built Swinton's "landship," and on September 15, 1916, Swinton rolled into battle leading 32 "tanks." The menacing, unstoppable appearance of these trucks frightened the enemy and impressed journalists. Tanks were the most innovative and successful military truck of the two world wars.

Viktor Schreckengost

Born in Ohio in 1906, Viktor Schreckengost studied ceramics. One of the first industrial designers, he founded

Viktor Schreckengost was an exceptional designer. He designed many products and also trained other industrial designers.

an industrial design school where he trained more than 1,000 designers. His students included design chiefs at major automotive corporations. His passion for beauty and function shows in his designs of toys, bicycles, furniture, tractors, flashlights, and more.

In 1933, Schreckengost helped produce the cab-over-engine truck design for the White Motor Company in Cleveland. The flat-front design helped manufacturers meet strict laws limiting truck length without sacrificing payload space. Cab-over-engine trucks are used extensively throughout Asia and Europe today.

Glossary

commercial (kuh-MUHR-shuhl) having to do with buying or selling things

compression (kuhm-PREH-shuhn) squeezed or pressed together

coupler (KUHP-luhr) something that joins or links two parts together

diesel engines (DEE-zuhl EHN-juhnz) internal combustion engines that rely on compression of air and use of thick fuel for ignition

efficient (ih-FIH-shuhnt) ability to make or do something desired without being wasteful

engines (EHN-juhnz) machines or motors that change energy into mechanical force

flexibility (flek-suh-BIHL-uh-tee) ability to adapt or change

forerunner (FOR-ruh-nuhr) something that has come before

ingenuity (ehn-juh-NOO-uh-tee) creativity or originality

internal combustion engine (ihn-TUHR-nuhl kuhm-BUHS-chuhn EHN-juhn) an engine that relies on the burning of fuel or fuel-air mixtures for ignition

patents (PAT-uhnts) legal documents giving an inventor the sole rights to manufacture and sell his or her invention

remedy (REH-muh-dee) to provide relief from

satellites (SAA-tuh-lites) objects that orbit Earth; some satellites receive or collect signals and send them back to Earth

For More Information

BOOKS

Nakaya, Andrea C., ed. *Cars in America*. San Diego: Greenhaven Press, 2006.

Shores, Erika L. *Henry Ford: A Photo-Illustrated Biography*. Mankato, MN: Bridgestone Books, 2004.

WEB SITES

America on the Move: Games
americanhistory.si.edu/onthemove/games/
Play games to learn more about transportation

Energy Information Administration: Kid's Page Transportation Timeline
www.eia.doe.gov/kids/history/timelines/transportation.html
Learn more about the history of transportation

Energy Quest: A Student's Guide to Alternative Fuel Vehicles
www.energyquest.ca.gov/transportation/index.html
Information about vehicles that use alternative fuels and links to related sites

Index

About the Author

Matt Mullins lives in Madison, Wisconsin, with his wife and son. Formerly a journalist, Matt writes about science and technology and, when time permits, on topics ranging from food and wine to current affairs. He holds a master's degree in the history of science from the University of Wisconsin–Madison. At this time, Matt does not own a truck, and this makes him sad.